MIDI AND ARDUINO:

ORGAN BASS PEDAL ENCODERS

TOM SCARFF

TABLE OF CONTENTS

Figures

Listings

Tables

PREFACE

This book contains designs for MIDI software and hardware, for Organ Bass Pedal Encoders ranging in size from 13 to 32 notes.

An Introduction to Organ Bass Pedals

1.1 Organ Bass Pedalboards

Organ Bass Pedalboards have been a standard feature on pipe organs for centuries, and produce sounds in the bass range, which, in organ terminology is the 16' stop. Some bass pedals have an 8' stop (an octave higher) which can be used by itself or combined with the 16' stop. Bass pedals are used by keyboard players as an addition to their full-range manual keyboards.

1.2 Types of Organ Bass Pedalboards

Electronic Bass pedal units usually have a smaller range (13 notes) than a church pipe organ's pedal keyboard (32 notes for an American Guild of Organists standard pedalboard). Bass pedals with larger ranges are less common, but do exist, such as 17 notes (C to E), 20 notes (C to G), and 25 notes (C to C two octaves higher). As well, bass pedals usually have shorter pedals than those on a church pipe organ's pedalboard.

1.3 Organ Bass Pedalboard Structure

Most bass pedal units consist of foot-operated pedals mounted in a chassis that sits on the floor. Often the chassis has buttons on top, also designed to be operated with the feet, which enable the performer to change the sound. Typical buttons include a 16' and 8' button to give a contrabass or bass sound.

The main identifying aspects of a pedalboard are the number of pedals, and whether all the pedals are at the same height relative to the floor ("flat"), or whether the pedals in the middle are lower than those on the outer edges, forming a curved-in shape ("concave"), and whether all the pedals are completely parallel to each other ("parallel"), or whether the pedals are closer together at the far end than at the end closest to the organ console ("radiating").

Specifications vary by country, organ builder, era, and individual tastes. Exact design specifications for pedalboards are published in Great Britain by the Royal College of Organists (RCO), in the United States by the American Guild of Organists (AGO), which requires a design similar to the RCO's, and in Germany by the Bund Deutscher Orgelbaumeister (BDO), which allows both 30 and 32-note pedalboards, of both concave/radiating and concave/parallel varieties.

1.4 History of Electronic Bass Pedalboards

Electronic Bass pedals serve the same function as the pedalboard on a pipe organ or an electric organ. Since the 1930s, electromechanical organs such as the Hammond organ often included pedalboards. In the 1960s, home organs by Hammond, Farfisa, and other manufacturers included short, 13-note bass pedals attached to the base of the chassis.

In the 1970s, electronic organ makers were aware that musicians wanted organs made more portable. The earliest bass pedals consisted of a pedalboard and analog synthesiser tone generation circuitry, packaged together as a unit. The bass pedals were plugged into a bass amplifier or PA system so that their sound could be heard.

A 1970s bass pedal is typically monophonic, which meant that it could only play one note at a time. Even if the player presses two pedals simultaneously, such as a C and a G, only one note sounds.

To make organs more portable, they were changed from being housed in heavy wooden consoles with an integrated amplifier and speaker and bass pedals to being made as a main keyboard, a detachable stand, and detachable bass pedals.

1.5 MIDI Organ Bass Pedalboards

Since the 1990s, bass pedals are usually MIDI controllers, which have to be connected to a MIDI-compatible computer, electronic synthesiser keyboard, or synthesiser module to produce musical tones. Some 2010s-era bass pedals have both an onboard synthesiser module and a MIDI output.

Some MIDI bass pedals designed to be used with electronic organs have a MIDI merge feature, so that one or more keyboards can have their MIDI outs plugged into the bass pedal, and then the bass pedal merges the MIDI messages and sends them, via the bass pedal's MIDI out, to the organ sound module. This function might be needed if a keyboardist had two MIDI controller keyboards, and the bass pedals, and wants the MIDI messages from all three controllers to be sent to the sound module.

Despite the fact that these pedalboards can control any kind of MIDI device, and can therefore produce a virtually unlimited range of musical pitches, ranging from a high-pitched melody to percussion sounds, they are still often referred to as "bass pedals".

These MIDI systems are less expensive than metal or wooden bass pipes, which are very costly to purchase and install, due to their heavy weight, large size, and need for large amounts of wind. Another rationale for using MIDI systems is that it may be easier to get a focused sound with a MIDI system, because all of the bass tone emanates from a single speaker or set of speakers. With traditional pipes, it can be difficult to give the pedal division a focused sound, because the large pipes tend to be spread out over the entire organ pipe chest.

1.6 Design of DIY MIDI Organ Bass Pedals

Since MIDI pedalboards are often very expensive, some amateur home organists make DIY MIDI pedalboards by retrofitting an old pedalboard with MIDI. Due to the popularity of organs during the 1950s and 1960s, many organ parts are available on the market, including pedalboards, for a relatively cheap price. After the pedalboard is cleaned up and glass reed switches are repaired or replaced, the pedal contacts can be soldered into these pedalboard MIDI encoder designs, which can then be connected to any MIDI device, to produce the sound of an organ or any other musical instrument.

An Introduction to MIDI

2.1 What is MIDI ?

MIDI is an acronym that stands for Musical Instrument Digital Interface. It is a technical standard digital communications protocol that allows computers, musical instruments and other hardware to connect audio devices together for playing, editing and recording music. MIDI also describes a digital interface, and electrical connectors for digital communication.

This allows one keyboard to trigger sounds on another synthesiser. Also virtual software synthesisers, which are computer programs that simulate hardware synthesisers, communicate with computer sequencing software running on the same computer using MIDI messages.

MIDI works as a digital signal. A series of binary digits (0s and 1s). Each instrument understands and then responds to these 1s and 0s, which are combined into 8-bit messages supporting data rates of up to 31,250 bits per second.

2.2 MIDI Channel and MIDI System Messages

MIDI messages consist of two main components:

1) MIDI Channel Messages,

2) MIDI System Messages.

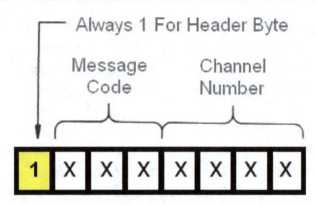

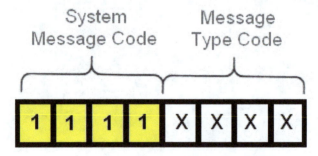

Figure 1: MIDI Channel and System Messages

The MIDI Channel Message Header Byte consists of a Message Code and a Channel Number. The Message Code 'xxx' can range from 000 to 110 in binary, which is 0 to 6 in decimal. So this allows for 7 different Channel Voice Message codes.The Channel Voice Messages are used to send musical performance information

The first half of the MIDI command byte (the three bits following the MSB) sets the type of command.

The 7 messages in this category are:

10000000 = Note Off,

10010000 = Note On,

10100000 = Aftertouch,

10110000 = Continuous Controller,

11000000 = Program Change,

11010000 = Channel Pressure,

11100000 = Pitch Bend.

The MIDI Channel Number 'xxxx' ranges in binary from 0000 to 1111, which is 0 to 15 in decimal. Note however that many MIDI systems often refer to these as MIDI Channels 1 to 16 (which can lead to some confusion).

The concept of channels is central to how most MIDI messages work. A channel is an independent path over which messages travel to their destination. There are 16 channels per MIDI device.

2.3 Organ Bass Pedal Note On Messages

In MIDI systems, the activation of a particular note and the release of the same note are considered as two separate events. When a pedal is pressed on a MIDI pedalboard instrument or MIDI pedalboard controller, the pedalboard sends a Note On message on the MIDI OUT port.

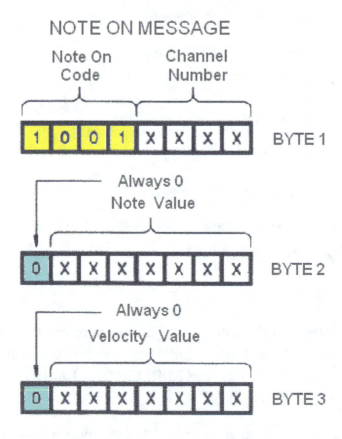

Figure 2: MIDI Note On Message

The pedalboard may be set to transmit on any one of the sixteen logical MIDI channels, and the status byte for the Note On message will indicate the selected channel number. The Note On status byte is followed by two data bytes, which specify pedal number (indicating which pedal was pressed) and velocity (how hard the pedal was pressed). The pedal number is used in the receiving synthesiser to select which note should be played, and the velocity is normally used to control the amplitude of the note.

The Note On Message consists of three 8-bit bytes. Byte 1 contains the Note On command code and the MIDI Channel Number. The Note On code is 1001 in binary, which is 144 in decimal and 0x90 in Hexadecimal.

The MIDI Channel Number 'xxxx' ranges in binary from 0000 to 1111, which is 0 to 15 in decimal, respectively. Note however that most MIDI systems often refer to these as MIDI Channels 1 to 16.

Byte 2 contains the Note Value xxxxxxx which ranges in value from 0000000 to 1111111 in binary, which is 0 to 127 in decimal and 0x00 to 0x7F in Hexadecimal.

Byte 3 contains the Velocity Value xxxxxxx which ranges in value from 0000000 to 1111111 in binary, which is 0 to 127 in decimal and 0x00 to 0x7F in Hexadecimal.

Generally the harder you 'hit' a pedal on a pedalboard the higher the velocity value, which produces a sound with a higher volume. Note though that some pedalboards do not measure the velocity and instead output a fixed velocity value. Also a velocity value of 0000000 is equivalent to a MIDI Note Off message and switches the note off.

2.4 Organ Bass Pedal Note Off Messages

When the pedal is released, the pedalboard instrument or controller will send a Note Off message. The Note Off message also includes data bytes for the pedal number and for the velocity with which the pedal was released.

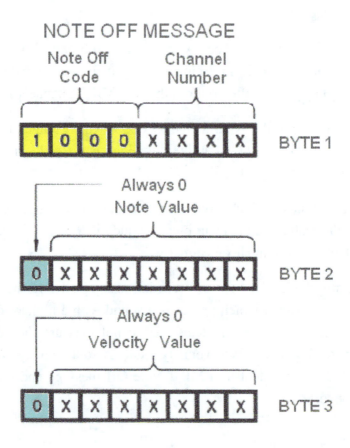

Figure 3: MIDI Note Off Message

The Note Off Message consists of three 8-bit bytes. Byte 1 contains the Note Off command code and the MIDI Channel Number. The Note Off code is 1000 in binary, which is 128 in decimal and 0x80 in Hexadecimal.

The MIDI Channel Number 'xxxx' ranges in binary from 0000 to 1111, which is 0 to 15 in decimal, respectively. . Note however that most MIDI systems often refer to these as MIDI Channels 1 to 16.

Byte 2 contains the Note Value xxxxxxx which ranges in value from 0000000 to 1111111 in binary, which is 0 to 127 in decimal and 0x00 to 0x7F in Hexadecimal.

Byte 3 contains the Velocity Value xxxxxxx which ranges in value from 0000000 to 1111111 in binary, which is 0 to 127 in decimal and 0x00 to 0x7F in Hexadecimal.

2.5 MIDI Note Numbers for Different Octaves

Octave notation is given here in the International Organization for Standardization ISO system, ISO was formed to include/replace the American National Standards Institute (ANSI) and Deutsches Institut für Normung (DIN), the German standards institute.

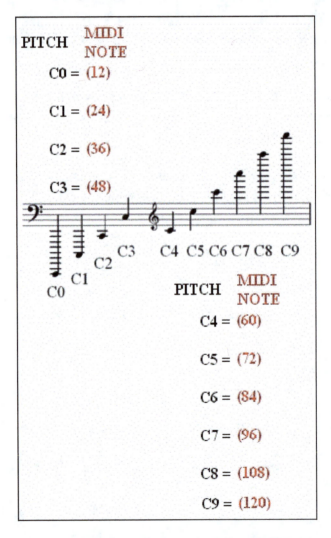

Figure 4: MIDI Note Numbers for Different Octaves

In this system, middle C (MIDI note number 60) is C4. A MIDI note number of 69 is used for A440 tuning, that is, the A note above middle C.

2.6 MIDI Note Numbers

The MIDI specification only defines note number 60 as "Middle C", and all other notes are relative. The absolute octave number designations shown here are based on Middle C = C4.

There is a discrepancy that occurs between various models of MIDI devices and software programs, and that concerns the octave numbers for note names. If your MIDI software/device considers octave 0 as being the lowest octave of the MIDI note range, then middle C's note name is C5. The lowest note name is then C0 (note number 0), and the highest possible note name is G10 (note number 127).

Some software/devices instead consider the third octave of the MIDI note range (2 octaves below middle C) as octave 0. In that case, the first 2 octaves are referred to as -2 and -1. So, middle C's note name is C3, the lowest note name is C-2, and the highest note name is G8.

A MIDI device can have up to 128 distinct pitches/notes, from 0 to 127 . But whereas musicians name the keys using the alphabetical names, with sharps and flats, and also octave numbers, this is more difficult for MIDI devices to process, so instead a unique number is assigned to each key.

Octave	Note Numbers											
	C	C#	D	D#	E	F	F#	G	G#	A	A#	B
-1	0	1	2	3	4	5	6	7	8	9	10	11
0	12	13	14	15	16	17	18	19	20	21	22	23
1	24	25	26	27	28	29	30	31	32	33	34	35
2	36	37	38	39	40	41	42	43	44	45	46	47
3	48	49	50	51	52	53	54	55	56	57	58	59
4	60	61	62	63	64	65	66	67	68	69	70	71
5	72	73	74	75	76	77	78	79	80	81	82	83
6	84	85	86	87	88	89	90	91	92	93	94	95
7	96	97	98	99	100	101	102	103	104	105	106	107
8	108	109	110	111	112	113	114	115	116	117	118	119
9	120	121	122	123	124	125	126	127				

Table 1: MIDI Note Numbers for different Octaves

The numbers used are 0 to 127. The lowest note upon a MIDI controller is a C and this is assigned note number 0. The C# above it would have a note number of 1. The D note above that would have a note number of 2. So "Middle C" is note number 60. A MIDI note number of 69 is used for A440 tuning, that is the A note above middle C.

MIDI Hardware

3.1 MIDI Hardware

A MIDI device is equipped with ports for MIDI IN, MIDI OUT and MIDI THRU. A special type of cable known as a MIDI cable is used to make these connections. Each wire is actually made of 3 wires, two are used for data transmission and one is a shield.

Each MIDI connection along one of these cables, can contain up to 16 channels of information and each MIDI device has 16 channels. Each one of these channels can have its own specified note, velocity, pitch bend etc.

It gets slightly confusing as MIDI signals can now be transferred via USB. This is common in most modern synthesisers or MIDI keyboards. The USB effectively takes the place of the In, Out and Thru ports.

3.2 The MIDI IN Port

The MIDI IN schematic circuit diagram consists of a 5-pin DIN 180 degree socket connected to, IC1, a 6N139 high speed opto-isolator, via, R1, a 220 ohm resistor. The input is wired in current loop mode which helps avoid earth loop problems. The IN4148 diode, D1, prevents reverse current problems to the opto-isolator, if an external MIDI cable is connected incorrectly.

The output of the opto-isolator is connected to the RX pin of the Arduino. The opto-isolator is also connected to the 5V (Volt) and GND (Ground) pins of the Arduino.

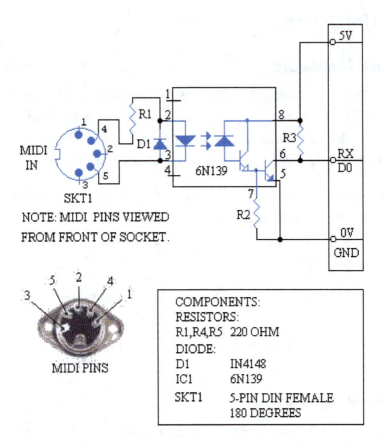

Figure 5: MIDI IN Schematic Drawing

3.3 MIDI IN and MIDI THRU Ports

The MIDI THRU schematic consists of the addition of two Schmitt-trigger Inverters to the MIDI IN circuit. The MIDI THRU design uses the SN74LS14N which is a Hex Schmitt-trigger Inverter, temperature compensated and can be triggered from the slowest of input ramps and still give clean, jitter-free output signals. Each circuit functions as an inverter, but because of the Schmitt action, it has different input threshold levels for positive-going (VT+) and negative-going (VT-) signals.

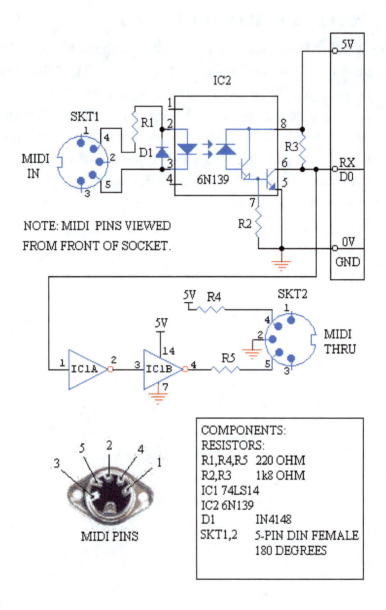

Figure 6: MIDI IN and THRU Schematic Drawing

3.4 MIDI OUT Port wiring

The MIDI OUT schematic circuit diagram consists of a 5-pin DIN 180 degree socket connected to two 220 ohm resistors. One of the 220 ohm resistors is connected to the +5 Volt (5V) pin of the Arduino and the other 220 ohm resistor is connected to the TX pin.

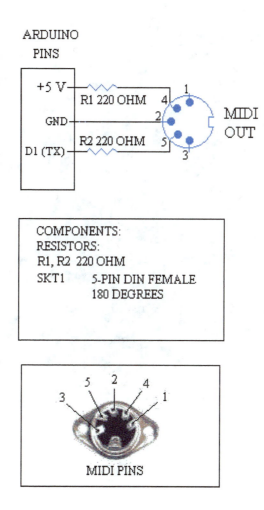

Figure 7: MIDI OUT Schematic Drawing

Pin 2 of the DIN socket is connected to the GND (GROUND) pin of the Arduino. This ground connection is usually connected to the screen of the MIDI cable which is connected to the MIDI socket. This is useful to prevent electrical interference being picked up from stray electrical fields along the cable length. The MIDI cable maximum length is specified as 15 metres.

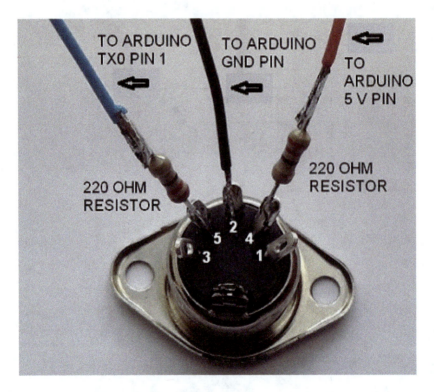

Figure 8: MIDI OUT Wiring Diagram

3.5 The Arduino MIDI IN/OUT Board

The Arduino MIDI IN/OUT board is designed so that it can be plugged into the Arduino Uno or Arduino Mega 2560 board directly and connect to digital pins D0 to D7, while still allowing access to all the other pins.

Figure 9: The Arduino MIDI IN/OUT Board

Pins D0 and D1 are connected to the RX and TX pins, respectively. Arduino Pins D2 and D3 require +5 Volt and 0 Volt(GND), respectively, and these voltages are provided in the software with these lines:

```
pinMode(2, OUTPUT);
pinMode(3, OUTPUT);
```

```
// GND 0 Volt supply to opto-coupler
  digitalWrite(3, LOW);
 // +5 Volt supply to opto-coupler
  digitalWrite(2, HIGH);
```

Then you need to set Arduino Pins D4, D5, D6 and D7, as digital input pins with internal pull-up resistors. These are connected to the 4-way DIL switch, to select the MIDI Channel (1 to 16), with these lines:

```
// Set Inputs for 4 way DIP Switch
  pinMode(4, INPUT_PULLUP);
  pinMode(5, INPUT_PULLUP);
  pinMode(6, INPUT_PULLUP);
  pinMode(7, INPUT_PULLUP);
```

The 4-way DIP switches are read, shifted and added to produce a sum between 0 and 15 for the MIDI Channel. However the Arduino MIDI Library software requires MIDI Channel values between 1 to 16. So 1 is added to the 'MIDIchannel' variable, as shown in this section of code:

```
// Read 4-way DIP switch
  MIDIchannel = digitalRead(4) + (digitalRead(5)
<< 1) + (digitalRead(6) << 2) + (digitalRead(7)
<< 3);
  MIDIchannel = MIDIchannel + 1;
```

The lines:

```
#include <MIDI.h>
MIDI_CREATE_DEFAULT_INSTANCE();
```

call the MIDI Library functions and initialises MIDI with:

```
MIDI.begin(MIDI_CHANNEL_OMNI);
```

The MIDI Channel is selected by the 4-way DIP switches.

DIP Switch Selections				MIDI
4	3	2	1	Channel
on	on	on	on	1
on	on	on	off	2
on	on	off	on	3
on	on	off	off	4
on	off	on	on	5
on	off	on	off	6
on	off	off	on	7
on	off	off	off	8
off	on	on	on	9
off	on	on	off	10
off	on	off	on	11
off	on	off	off	12
off	off	on	on	13
off	off	on	off	14
off	off	off	on	15
off	off	off	off	16
MIDI Channel Selection				

Table 2: DIP switch MIDI channel (1-16) setting

The 4-way DIP switches are a set of electrical switches packaged in a small box or housing. They are designed to be mounted on printed circuit boards to provide a range of electrical inputs to an electronic device based on the position of the individual switches. Each of the 4 switches can be set to the On or Off position. With the 4 switches you have 16 different selections, as shown in Table 3. The switches can be used for the selection of a MIDI Channel from 1 to 16.

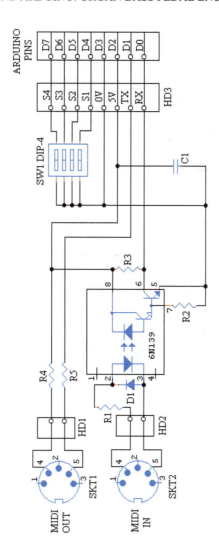

Figure 10: MIDI IN and OUT circuit Schematic Drawing

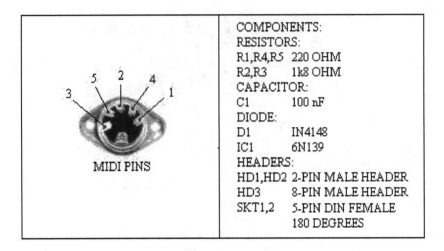

	COMPONENTS:
	RESISTORS:
	R1,R4,R5 220 OHM
	R2,R3 1k8 OHM
MIDI PINS	CAPACITOR:
	C1 100 nF
	DIODE:
	D1 IN4148
	IC1 6N139
	HEADERS:
	HD1,HD2 2-PIN MALE HEADER
	HD3 8-PIN MALE HEADER
	SKT1,2 5-PIN DIN FEMALE
	180 DEGREES

Figure 11: Components for.the MIDI IN and OUT circuit

3.6 Arduino MIDI IN/OUT Library Installation

The MIDI IN/OUT board requires the software from the Arduino MIDI Library, which is available at:

https://www.arduino.cc/reference/en/libraries/midi-library/

This library is compatible with all architectures so you should be able to use it on all the Arduino boards. To use this library, open the Library Manager in the Arduino IDE and install it from there:

https://www.arduino.cc/en/Guide/Libraries

An Introduction to the Arduino

4.1 What is the Arduino?

The Arduino is an open-source electronics platform based on easy-to-use hardware and software.Arduino designs and manufactures single-board microcontrollers and microcontroller kits for building digital devices. The Arduino single-board microcontroller boards are able to read inputs, make decisions and produce outputs. The Arduino board can be programmed by sending a set of instructions to the microcontroller on the board. To do so you use the Arduino programming language (based on Wiring), and the Arduino Software IDE (Integrated Development Environment), based on Processing.

4.2 Arduino Board Types

There are a large number of Arduino boards available. The 2 board types used for the Organ Bass Pedals projects are the Arduino UNO and the Arduino MEGA 2560.

Arduino board designs use a variety of microprocessors and microcontrollers. The boards are equipped with sets of digital and analog input/output (I/O) pins that may be interfaced to various expansion boards and other circuits. The boards feature serial communications interfaces, including Universal Serial Bus (USB) on some models, which are also used for loading programs.

4.3 Arduino Board Description

Some boards have different features from those given below, but most Arduinos have the majority of these components in common:

Reset Button – This will restart any code that is loaded to the Arduino board,

AREF – Stands for "Analog Reference" and is used to set an external reference voltage,

Ground Pin – There are a few ground pins on the Arduino,

Digital Input/Output – Pins 0-13 can be used for digital input or output,

PWM – The pins marked with the (~) symbol can simulate analog output,

USB Connection – Used for powering up the Arduino and uploading sketches,

ATmega Microcontroller – This is the brains and is where the programs are stored,

Crystal Oscillator – The crystal oscillator sets the basic time of operation of the Arduino. The number printed on top of the Arduino crystal is 16.000Hz, which is a frequency of 16,000,000 Hertz or 16 MHz,

Power LED Indicator – This LED lights up anytime the board is plugged in a power source,

DC Power Barrel Jack – This is used for powering your Arduino with a power supply,

Voltage Regulator – The function of the voltage regulator is to control the voltage sent to the Arduino board and stabilize the DC voltages used by the processor and other elements,

3.3V Pin – This pin supplies 3.3 volts of power to your projects,

5V Pin – This pin supplies 5 volts of power to your projects,

Analog Pins – These pins can read the signal from an analog sensor and convert it to digital data.

ICSP pins – The ICSP is a tiny programming header for the Arduino consisting of MOSI, MISO, SCK, RESET, VCC, and GND. It is often referred to as an SPI (Serial Peripheral Interface), which could be considered as an "expansion" of the output,

TX and RX LEDs – On the board, there are two labels: TX (transmit) and RX (receive). They appear in two places on the Arduino UNO board. First, at the digital pins 0 and 1, to indicate the pins responsible for serial communication. Second, the TX and RX led. The TX led flashes with different speed while sending the serial data. The speed of flashing depends on the baud rate used by the board. RX flashes during the receiving process.

The Arduino Uno needs a power source in order for it to operate and can be powered in a variety of ways. You can connect the board directly to your computer via a USB cable. If you want your project to be mobile, you can use a 9V battery pack to give it power. The last method would be to use a 9V DC power supply.

4.4 Arduino Installation

First you must have an Arduino board and a USB cable. In case you use Arduino UNO, Arduino Duemilanove, Nano, Arduino Mega 2560, or Diecimila, you will need a standard USB cable (A plug to B plug), the kind you would connect to a USB printer.

You can get different versions of the Arduino IDE from the Download page on the Arduino Official website, at:

https://www.arduino.cc/en/software

You then select the software, which is compatible with your operating system (Windows, IOS, or Linux). After your file download is complete, unzip the file.

The Arduino Software (IDE) allows you to write programs and upload them to your board. In the Arduino Software page you will find two options:

If you have a reliable Internet connection, you could use the online IDE (Arduino Web Editor). It will allow you to save your sketches in the cloud, having them available from any device and backed up. You will always have the most up-to-date version of the IDE without the need to install updates or community generated libraries. If you would rather work offline, you should use the latest version of the desktop IDE.

Then you power up the board. The Arduino Uno, Mega, Duemilanove and Arduino Nano automatically draw power from either, the USB connection to the computer or an external power supply.

After your Arduino IDE software is downloaded, you need to unzip the folder. Inside the folder, you can find the application icon with an infinity label (application.exe). Double-click the icon to start the IDE.

Now launch the Arduino IDE. Once the software starts, you can Create a new project or Open an existing project example. To create a new project, select File → New. To open an existing project example, select File → Example → Basics → Blink.

This is just one of the program examples called "Blink". It turns the LED on and off with some time delay. You can select any other example from the list.

MIDI AND ARDUINO: ORGAN BASS PEDAL ENCODERS

Then you select your Arduino board. To avoid any error while uploading your program to the board, you must select the correct Arduino board name, which matches with the board connected to your computer.

Go to the Menu → Tools → Board and select your board. Then you select the name matching the board that you are using.

Next select the serial device of the Arduino board. Go to Tools → Serial Port menu. This is likely to be COM3 or higher (COM1 and COM2 are usually reserved for hardware serial ports). To find out, you can disconnect your Arduino board and re-open the menu, the entry that disappears should be of the Arduino board. Reconnect the board and select that serial port.

Now, simply click the "Upload" button in the environment. Wait a few seconds; you will see the RX and TX LEDs on the board, flashing. If the upload is successful, the message "Done uploading" will appear in the status bar.

Note: If you are Uploading an Arduino program you need to make sure that the MIDI IN cable is not connected, as MIDI IN uses the same serial pin (RX) on the Arduino, and will prevent the program data from uploading. If you leave the MIDI OUT connected the program will upload fine, but be aware that you will be sending random MIDI data to the external MIDI device, which can cause problems. For example it may change the sounds in a synthesiser memory bank.

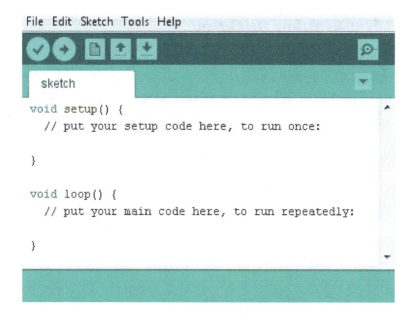

Listing 1: Simplest Arduino Sketch

This code contains two functions:

The first one is setup(). Anything you put in this function will be executed by the Arduino just once when the program starts.

The second one is loop(). Once the Arduino finishes with the code in the setup() function, it will move into a loop(), and it will continue running it in a loop, again and again, until you reset it or cut off the power.

Notice that both setup() and loop() have open and close parenthesis. Functions can receive parameters, which is a way by which the program can pass data between its different functions. The setup and loop functions don't have any parameters passed to them. Every single sketch you write will have these two functions in it, even if you don't use them.

4.5 The Arduino UNO Rev 3

The Arduino Uno is a microcontroller board based on the ATmega328P. It has 14 digital input/output pins (of which 6 can be used as PWM outputs), 6 analog inputs, a 16 MHz ceramic resonator, a USB connection, a power jack, an ICSP header and a reset button. It contains everything needed to support the microcontroller; simply connect it to a computer with a USB cable or power it with a AC-to-DC adapter or battery to get started.

Full information on the Arduino UNO Rev 3 is available at:

https://docs.arduino.cc/hardware/uno-rev3

Microcontroller	ATmega328P
Operating Voltage	5V
Input Voltage (recommended)	7-12V
Input Voltage (limit)	6-20V
Digital I/O Pins	14 (of which 6 provide PWM output)
PWM Digital I/O Pins	6
Analog Input Pins	6
DC Current per I/O Pin	20 mA
DC Current for 3.3V Pin	50 mA
Flash Memory	32 KB (ATmega328P) of which 0.5 KB used by bootloader
SRAM	2 KB (ATmega328P)
EEPROM	1 KB (ATmega328P)
Clock Speed	16 MHz
LED_BUILTIN	13
Length	68.6 mm
Width	53.4 mm
Weight	25 g

Table 3: The Arduino UNO Specifications

4.6 The Arduino MEGA 2560

The Arduino Mega 2560 is a microcontroller board based on the ATmega2560. It has 54 digital input/output pins (of which 15 can be used as PWM outputs), 16 analog inputs, 4 UARTs (hardware serial ports), a 16 MHz crystal oscillator, a USB connection, a power jack, an ICSP header, and a reset button.

Full information on the Arduino Mega 2560 is available at:

https://www.arduino.cc/en/Guide/ArduinoMega2560

Microcontroller	ATmega2560
Operating Voltage	5V
Input Voltage (recommended)	7-12V
Input Voltage (limit)	6-20V
Digital I/O Pins	54 (15 provide PWM output)
Analog Input Pins	16
DC Current per I/O Pin	20 mA
DC Current for 3.3V Pin	50 mA
Flash Memory	256 KB, with 8 K bootloader
SRAM	8 KB
EEPROM	4 KB
Clock Speed	16 MHz
LED_BUILTIN	13
Length	101.52 mm
Width	53.3 mm
Weight	37 g

Table 4: Arduino Mega 2560 Specifications

ARDUINO TESTING

5.1 Arduino Software and Hardware Testing

For projects that combine software and hardware it is good practice to be able to have simple programs to enable the testing of both elements. One simple example is to program the Arduino microcontroller board with a program to switch the internal LED (Light Emitting Diode) On and Off. This tests that the program has been uploaded correctly and that the LED hardware is also working.

5.2 Arduino LED Test Blink program

The main functionalities of the 'Blink' program are:

- Set pin 13 to an Output (do this once)

- Turn on the LED

- Wait for one second

- Turn off the LED

- Wait for one second

- Repeat turning LED on and off.

```
//  Blinking LED
// Turns on an LED on for one second, then off for
one second,
// repeatedly.

const int LED = 13;
// the setup function runs once when you press reset
or power on // the board
```

```
void setup() {
// initialize digital pin 13 as an output.
  pinMode(LED, OUTPUT);
}


// the loop function runs over and over again
forever
void loop() {
// turn the LED on (HIGH is the voltage level)
  digitalWrite(LED, HIGH);
  delay(1000);                   // wait for a second
// turn the LED off by making the voltage LOW
  digitalWrite(LED, LOW);
  delay(1000);                   // wait for a second
}
```

Listing 2: Blink Program for On-board LED

ARDUINO MIDI PROGRAMS

6.1 MIDI Software and Hardware Requirements

There are a number of items which may be needed for testing the MIDI Software and Hardware, such as:

An Arduino board, a cable type male USB A to male USB B, for programming or powering the Arduino board. A MIDI/USB cable or a MIDI/USB interface unit, to connect the MIDI OUT to a computer. Some designs require the MIDI IN, MIDI OUT or MIDI THRU hardware ports. A MIDI hardware or software synthesiser or MIDI module.

Figure 12: An Arduino Uno Board and male USB A to male USB B cable

Figure 13: A MIDI/USB Interface Cable

The Arduino UNO and Mega 2560 boards can be powered from the USB socket or via the external power connector. External power can come either from an AC-to-DC adapter or battery. The adapter can be connected by plugging a centre-positive plug with an internal diameter of 2.1mm, an external diameter of 5.5mm and 12mm long, into the board's power jack. Leads from a battery can be inserted in the Gnd and Vin pin headers of the POWER connector. A low dropout regulator provides improved energy efficiency.

The board can operate on an external supply of 7 to 20 volts. If supplied with less than 7V, however, the 5V pin may supply less than five volts and the board may be unstable. If using more than 12V, the voltage regulator may overheat and damage the board. The recommended range is 7 to 12 volts, capable of supplying about 1 Amp, which is 12 Watt (W) with a 12 Volt supply.. Note that the power input selection is automatically selected.

6.2 MIDI Monitoring

Note that MIDI operates at a BAUD rate of 31250, which is not one of the available choices in the Arduino Serial Monitor screen. So MIDI needs to be monitored with a special MIDI program.

Pocket MIDI is a MIDI monitoring tool for Windows and Mac. Connect your MIDI instrument to computer using a USB or USB/MIDI adapter and you can monitor MIDI messages to and from your instrument in real time. You can also send message from the application to your instrument. Pocket MIDI(for Windows/Mac) is freeware.

https://www.morson.jp/pocketmidi-webpage/

MidiView is a simple MIDI Monitor app, for Windows and Mac, that shows bi-directional MIDI packages that flow through your computer.

https://hautetechnique.com/midi/midiview/

MIDI-OX is a Windows 32 bit program., the world's greatest all-purpose MIDI Utility!

http://www.midiox.com/

Midi Monitoris a powerful tool to learn about Midi, to setup a Midi configuration and to exchange Midi System exclusive data. Midi channel messages real time monitoring.

http://obds.free.fr/midimon/

MIDI Monitor (Mac only) is an app to display MIDI signals going in and out of your Mac. Musicians will find it handy for tracking down confusing MIDI problems, and programmers can use it to test MIDI drivers and applications. MIDI Monitor is free to download and use.

https://www.snoize.com/midimonitor/

6.3 MIDI Organ Software Synthesisers

There are many software MIDI synthesisers available online. But probably the most popular MIDI Organ software synthesisers are Hauptwerk:

https://www.hauptwerk.com/

which is a computer program, designed to allow the playback or live performance of pipe organ music using MIDI, which is available for PC Windows and Mac OS X. Also GrandOrgue:

https://grandorgue.de/

which is a computer based pipe organ simulator. It enables you to play and hear the sound of many popular pipe organs. The software GrandOrgue was built under a free license, so you may download it from the web and use it for FREE! It is available for Microsoft Windows, Mac OS X, and Linux.

There is a wiki available for GrandOrgue at:

https://sourceforge.net/p/ourorgan/wiki/Home/

6.4 MIDI IN to OUT Activity Detector LED

This program lights the onboard LED whenever it detects MIDI IN activity on the RX pin. It also sends transfers the MIDI Input data to the Output TX Pin. So this tests the input and output pins for correct MIDI transmission.

```
// MIDI IN Activity Detector
// Program requires the MIDI IN and OUT
hardware

 #define LedPin 13

byte midiByte;

void setup() {
  pinMode(LedPin, OUTPUT);
  digitalWrite(LedPin, LOW);
  Serial.begin(31250); // set MIDI baud rate
  Serial.flush();
}

void loop() {
  if (Serial.available() > 0) {
    digitalWrite(LedPin, HIGH);
    // read the incoming byte:
    midiByte = Serial.read();
    // send the byte to the output
    Serial.write(midiByte);
    delay(1);
    digitalWrite(LedPin, LOW);
  }
}
```

Listing 3: MIDI IN Activity Detector

Note:When uploading the MIDI Activity Detector program make sure to disconnect the MIDI IN socket, because it uses the same RX Arduino Pin which is used for programming the Arduino. If the MIDI IN connection is not removed, then trying to program the Arduino will fail.

The program consists of three parts. The first part is where we 'declare' our constants and variables, the second part is the section of code called void setup(), and the third is the void loop().

All code between the curly brackets after the void setup() will be executed once, at the start of the program. All code between the curly brackets after void loop() will be executed repeatedly (after void setup() has run) until the program is stopped.

The statements:

```
pinMode(LedPin, OUTPUT);
digitalWrite(LedPin, LOW);
```

make the LedPin an Output and turns the LedPin LOW, which means the LED will be Off.

The statements:

```
Serial.begin(31250); // set MIDI baud rate
Serial.flush();
```

sets the Serial Output to the MIDI Baud rate of 31250 and then clears the Serial output.

The statement:

```
if (Serial.available() > 0) {
```

tests to see if any incoming MIDI data is available. If MIDI data is available the data is read using

```
midiByte = Serial.read();
```

and then the variable 'midiByte' is written to the TX port, using:

```
Serial.write(midiByte);
```

Organ Bass Pedal MIDI Encoders

7.1 An Introduction to Organ Bass Pedal MIDI Encoders

There are many different sizes of pedalboards available today. But generally pedalboards range in size from 13 notes on small organs designed for in-home use (an octave, conventionally C2 to C3) to 32 notes (two and a half octaves, C2 to G4) on church or concert organs. Modern pipe organs typically have 30-note or 32-note pedalboards, while some electronic organs and many older pipe organs have 25-note pedalboards.

These Organ Bass pedal MIDI encoder circuits use either the Arduino UNO or the Arduino 2560 board. Some of the designs are MIDI Out only and require the MIDI Out hardware circuit. Other designs have MIDI IN and OUT and use the MIDI IN/OUT board. These designs merge the MIDI IN data with the internal board data generated from the Bass pedal switches and send the combined MIDI data to the MIDI OUT socket. So they can be used in MIDI 'daisy-chain' mode to combine different MIDI devices.

The MIDI Output velocity is set to a fixed value of 100 to avoid problems due to the fact that you don't have the same mobility in your feet as in your hands. Also the pedal part is usually not called upon to play fast, complex music with lots of skips.

External power, for all the Organ Bass pedal MIDI encoder circuits, can come either from the USB socket, an AC-to-DC adapter or a battery.

7.2 Magnetic Reed Switches for Organ Bass Pedal MIDI Encoders

Magnetic reed switches can be used in all the designs, either to replace the original pedalboard switches or to work effectively in parallel with them. This would allow older electronic pedalboards that contain working electronics to have the old original electronics working at the same time as the new MIDI encoder, without electrical interference from each other.

There are many sizes or reed switch available so it is best to get a size that is suitable for your particular pedalboard. Also the magnets are available in different sizes and strengths. So when testing the system out you need to adjust the position of the magnets so that the switches operate correctly. Sometimes if the magnets are too strong or positioned incorrectly they can accidently operate adjacent reed switches.

The reed switches required for all the MIDI designs need to be Normally Open (N.O.). So they only close and make contact when the magnet moves close to them. Normally the magnet is glued to the moving part of the pedal and the reed switch is wired to the non-moving part of the pedalboard structure.

A 13-Note Organ Bass Pedal MIDI Encoder

This design uses an Arduino UNO board and the MIDI OUT hardware. The MIDI Bass Pedal Encoder circuit is capable of encoding 13 momentary action, push to make, single pole single throw (SPST), switches to produce the equivalent MIDI note-on/note-off data commands.

Figure 14: Arduino UNO Board with MIDI Out Wiring

One side of each of the encoded Bass Pedal switches are wired to a common Ground (GND) pin and the other side of each switch is wired to a different digital input pin. The MIDI start Note is set to C2 (MIDI Note 36), which is connected to switch SW1, then the switches follow continuously to the last switch SW13, which is C3

(MIDI Note 48). But any different start note can be pre-programmed if required.

8.1 Operation

This unit can work standard MIDI Baud rate of 31250. This unit can be connected to new bass pedals or it can be used with older non-MIDI bass pedals, by using magnetic/reed switches to isolate the old and new scanning circuits. This will allow the older bass pedal synthesiser to continue to operate as normal while also providing a MIDI output, at the same time.

8.2 Features

The MIDI 13 Note Organ Bass Pedal Encoder Unit consists of an a MIDI Arduino UNO Board, the MIDI channel is preset to channel 3, the velocity byte is preset to a value of 100, the start note of the bass pedal encoder is from MIDI note C2 (MIDI Note 36), a 2.1mm power socket, and associated LED, a MIDI 5-pin DIN output socket and associated series 220 ohm resistors, a 9v battery or equivalent DC power source, or it can be powered via the USB socket, 13 suitable key-switches or magnetic reed switches.

8.3 Source code for a 13 Note Organ Bass Pedal Encoder

```
// A design with a 13 switch encoder circuit to
// produce 13 note Bass pedal outputs

// define the 13 input pins
#define Switch0 2
#define Switch1 3
#define Switch2 8
#define Switch3 9
```

```
#define Switch4 10
#define Switch5 11
#define Switch6 12
#define Switch7 14
#define Switch8 15
#define Switch9 16
#define Switch10 17
#define Switch11 18
#define Switch12 19

//variables setup

byte MIDIchannel = 2; // midi channel 3
byte x;
byte LedPin = 13;   // select the pin for the
LED

byte count;
byte note;
byte velocity = 100;
byte currentSwitch = 0;
int startNote = 36;

byte switches[13] = {
 Switch0, Switch1, Switch2, Switch3, Switch4,
Switch5, Switch6, Switch7, Switch8, Switch9,
Switch10, Switch11, Switch12
};

byte switchState[13] = {
  LOW, LOW, LOW, LOW, LOW, LOW, LOW, LOW, LOW,
LOW, LOW, LOW, LOW
};

//-----------------------------------------------
-----
void setup() {

  pinMode(Switch0, INPUT_PULLUP);
  pinMode(Switch1, INPUT_PULLUP);
  pinMode(Switch2, INPUT_PULLUP);
  pinMode(Switch3, INPUT_PULLUP);
  pinMode(Switch4, INPUT_PULLUP);
```

```
  pinMode(Switch5, INPUT_PULLUP);
  pinMode(Switch6, INPUT_PULLUP);
  pinMode(Switch7, INPUT_PULLUP);
  pinMode(Switch8, INPUT_PULLUP);
  pinMode(Switch9, INPUT_PULLUP);
  pinMode(Switch10, INPUT_PULLUP);
  pinMode(Switch11, INPUT_PULLUP);
  pinMode(Switch12, INPUT_PULLUP);

  // declare the LED's pin as output
  pinMode(LedPin, OUTPUT);

  for (x = 1; x <= 4; x++) {  // Flash LED 4
times
    digitalWrite( LedPin, HIGH );
    delay(300);
    digitalWrite( LedPin, LOW );
    delay(300);
  }

  Serial.begin(31250);  //start serial with
midi baudrate 31250
  Serial.flush();

}
//------------------------------------------------
void loop() {

  // scan 13 switches on inputs
  for (int n = 0; n < 13; n++) {
    currentSwitch = digitalRead(switches[n]);

// switch pressed and NOT pressed previously
    if ( currentSwitch == LOW && switchState[n]
== LOW) {        switchState[n] = HIGH;
      note = n;
      noteOn(MIDIchannel, note, velocity);
    }

// switch released and pressed previously
    if ( currentSwitch == HIGH &&
switchState[n] == HIGH ) {        switchState[n]
= LOW;
```

```
        note = n;
        noteOff(MIDIchannel, note, velocity);
      }
    }
// short delay for switch debouncing
    delay(20);


}
//---------------------------------------------

// Send a MIDI note-on message.
void noteOn(byte channel, byte note, byte
velocity) {
    midiMsg( (0x90 + channel), note + startNote,
velocity);
}

// Send a MIDI note-off message.
void noteOff(byte channel, byte note, byte
velocity) {
    midiMsg( (0x80 + channel), note + startNote,
velocity);
}

// Send a general MIDI message
void midiMsg(byte cmd, byte data1, byte data2)
{
    digitalWrite(LedPin, HIGH); // indicate we're
sending MIDI data
    Serial.write(cmd);
    Serial.write(data1);
    Serial.write(data2);
    digitalWrite(LedPin, LOW);
}
```

Listing 4: A 13 Note Organ Bass Pedal Encoder

8.4 Explanation of the source code

The 13 Pins on the Arduino used for switch Inputs are defined by:

```
#define Switch0 2
#define Switch1 3
#define Switch2 8
#define Switch3 9
#define Switch4 10
#define Switch5 11
#define Switch6 12
#define Switch7 14
#define Switch8 15
#define Switch9 16
#define Switch10 17
#define Switch11 18
#define Switch12 19
```

The byte switches[13] Array stores the 13 switches

```
byte switches[13] = {
 Switch0, Switch1, Switch2, Switch3, Switch4,
Switch5, Switch6, Switch7, Switch8, Switch9,
Switch10, Switch11, Switch12
};
```

The byte switchState[13] Array stores the initial state of all 13 switches

```
byte switchState[13] = {
  LOW, LOW, LOW, LOW, LOW, LOW, LOW, LOW, LOW,
LOW, LOW, LOW, LOW
};
```

The 13 switches are made Digital Inputs, connected to an internal Pull Up resistor by:

```
  pinMode(Switch0, INPUT_PULLUP);
  pinMode(Switch1, INPUT_PULLUP);
  pinMode(Switch2, INPUT_PULLUP);
```

```
pinMode(Switch3, INPUT_PULLUP);
pinMode(Switch4, INPUT_PULLUP);
pinMode(Switch5, INPUT_PULLUP);
pinMode(Switch6, INPUT_PULLUP);
pinMode(Switch7, INPUT_PULLUP);
pinMode(Switch8, INPUT_PULLUP);
pinMode(Switch9, INPUT_PULLUP);
pinMode(Switch10, INPUT_PULLUP);
pinMode(Switch11, INPUT_PULLUP);
pinMode(Switch12, INPUT_PULLUP);
```

Then the LED on Pin 13 of the board is set as an Output:

```
// declare the LED's pin as output
pinMode(LedPin, OUTPUT);
```

Then the LED on Pin 13 of the board is flashed 4 times:

```
for (x = 1; x <= 4; x++) {  // Flash LED 4 times
    digitalWrite( LedPin, HIGH );
    delay(300);
    digitalWrite( LedPin, LOW );
    delay(300);
}
```

The statements:

```
Serial.begin(31250); // set MIDI baud rate
Serial.flush();
```

sets the Serial Output to the MIDI Baud rate of 31250 and then clears the Serial output.

The FOR Loop goes from n = 0 to n = 12 in increments of +1 steps. This provides a pointer to the Array of switches so that each switch can be tested:

```
for (int n = 0; n < 13; n++) {
```

Then with each step of the FOR Loop the current switch is read and then tested:

```
currentSwitch = digitalRead(switches[n]);
```

The switch is tested by:

```
// switch pressed and NOT pressed previously
    if ( currentSwitch == LOW && switchState[n]
== LOW)
```

which checks if the switch is pressed AND not pressed previously, and then

```
{       switchState[n] = HIGH;
      note = n;
      noteOn(MIDIchannel, note, velocity);
    }
```

Sets the `switchState[n] = HIGH;` and calls the `noteOn` function.

Then the switch is tested by:

```
// switch released and pressed previously
    if ( currentSwitch == HIGH && switchState[n]
== HIGH )
```

Then the `switchState[n]` is set LOW and the `noteOff` function is called:

```
{       switchState[n] = LOW;
      note = n;
      noteOff(MIDIchannel, note, velocity);
    }
```

Then there is a short delay for switch de-bouncing:
```
// short delay for switch debouncing
  delay(20);
```

which is a 20 millisecond delay to prevent false switch triggers.

The noteOn function:

```
// Send a MIDI note-on message.
void noteOn(byte channel, byte note, byte
velocity) {
  midiMsg( (0x90 + channel), note + startNote,
velocity);
}
```

sends a series of 3 bytes to the MIDI OUT socket. Firstly the Note On command of 0x90 added to the channel, then the note (0 to 12) added to the startNote and lastly the velocity byte.

The noteOff function:

```
// Send a MIDI note-off message.
void noteOff(byte channel, byte note, byte
velocity) {
  midiMsg( (0x80 + channel), note + startNote,
velocity);
}
```

sends a series of 3 bytes to the MIDI OUT socket. Firstly the Note Off command of 0x80 added to the channel, then the note (0 to 12) added to the startNote and lastly the velocity byte.

Finally the MIDI data is written to the Serial TX Output with:

```
// Send a general MIDI message
void midiMsg(byte cmd, byte data1, byte data2) {
  digitalWrite(LedPin, HIGH);
  Serial.write(cmd);
  Serial.write(data1);
  Serial.write(data2);
  digitalWrite(LedPin, LOW);
}
```

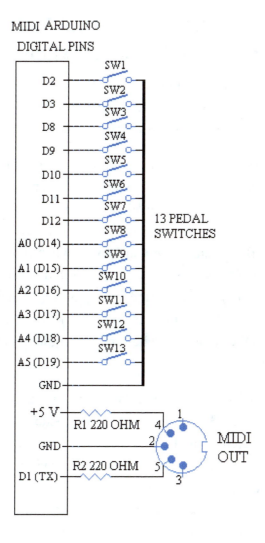

Figure 15: A 13 Note Organ Bass Pedal Encoder schematic

A 13-Note Organ Bass Pedal MIDI Encoder with Octave and Channel Switch Inputs

This design is similar to the previous 13 note bass pedal encoder, and uses the Arduino UNO board and the MIDI OUT hardware, but with the addition of 4 switch inputs.

This MIDI Bass Pedal Encoder circuit is capable of encoding 13 momentary action, push to make, single pole single throw (SPST), switches to produce the equivalent MIDI note-on/note-off data commands. There are also Octave Up and Octave Down switch inputs and MIDI Channel Up and Down switch inputs. The MIDI Channel and Octave Selection are stored into non-volatile EEPROM memory. So when the unit is powered up the previous MIDI Channel that was used is restored. Note that if the MIDI Octave or MIDI Channel switches are not required, they can be left unconnected.

One side of each of the encoded Bass Pedal switches are wired to a common Ground (GND) pin and the other side of each switch is wired to a different digital input pin. The MIDI start Note is set to C2 (MIDI Note 36), which is connected to switch SW1, then the switches follow continuously to the last switch SW13, which is C3 (MIDI Note 48). But any different start note can be pre-programmed if required.

9.1 Operation

This unit can work with the standard MIDI Baud rate of 31250. This unit can be connected to new bass pedals or it can be used with older non-MIDI bass pedals by using magnetic/reed switches to isolate the old and new scanning circuits. This will allow the older bass pedal synthesiser to continue to operate as normal, while also providing a MIDI output.

9.2 Features

The MIDI 13 Note Bass Pedal Encoder Unit consists of a MIDI Arduino Uno Board, the MIDI channel is preset to channel 3, the velocity byte is preset to a value of 100, the start note of the bass pedal encoder is from MIDI note C2 (MIDI Note 36), Octave Up and Octave Down switch inputs, the Octave Selection is stored into non-volatile EEPROM memory, MIDI Channel Up and MIDI Channel Down switch inputs, the MIDI Channel is stored into non-volatile EEPROM memory, a 2.1mm power socket, and associated LED, a MIDI 5-pin DIN output socket and associated series resistors. a 9v battery or equivalent DC power source or powered via the USB socket, 13 suitable key-switches or magnetic reed switches, suitable 2 momentary action Octave Up/Down switches, suitable 2 momentary action MIDI Channel Up/Down switches.

9.3 Source code for a 13-Note Bass Pedal MIDI Encoder with Octave and Channel Switch Inputs

```
/*
  A MIDI Organ Bass Pedal design with a 13
switch encoder circuit, with Octave UP/DOWN
switches, and with MIDI Channel UP/DOWN
switches, to produce a MIDI output.
*/

#include <EEPROM.h>

// define the input pins
#define Switch0 2
#define Switch1 3
#define Switch2 8
#define Switch3 9
#define Switch4 10
#define Switch5 11
#define Switch6 12
```

```
#define Switch7 14
#define Switch8 15
#define Switch9 16
#define Switch10 17
#define Switch11 18
#define Switch12 19

//variables setup
int octave = 0;
int MIDIchannel = 2; // midi channel 3
byte channel;
byte x;
byte LedPin = 13;   // select the pin for the
LED

byte count;
byte note;
byte velocity = 100;
byte currentSwitch = 0;
int startNote = 36;

byte switches[17] = {
  2, 3, 8, 9, 10, 11, 12, 14, 15, 16, 17, 18,
19, 4, 5, 6, 7
};

byte switchState[17] = {
  0, 0, 0, 0, 0, 0, 0, 0, 0, 0, 0, 0, 0, 0, 0,
0, 0
};

void setup() {
 // Set Inputs for Octave up/down Switches
  pinMode(4, INPUT_PULLUP);
  pinMode(5, INPUT_PULLUP);
 // Set Inputs for MIDI Channel up/down
Switches
  pinMode(6, INPUT_PULLUP);
  pinMode(7, INPUT_PULLUP);

  pinMode(Switch0, INPUT_PULLUP);
  pinMode(Switch1, INPUT_PULLUP);
  pinMode(Switch2, INPUT_PULLUP);
```

```
  pinMode(Switch3, INPUT_PULLUP);
  pinMode(Switch4, INPUT_PULLUP);
  pinMode(Switch5, INPUT_PULLUP);
  pinMode(Switch6, INPUT_PULLUP);
  pinMode(Switch7, INPUT_PULLUP);
  pinMode(Switch8, INPUT_PULLUP);
  pinMode(Switch9, INPUT_PULLUP);
  pinMode(Switch10, INPUT_PULLUP);
  pinMode(Switch11, INPUT_PULLUP);
  pinMode(Switch12, INPUT_PULLUP);

  pinMode(LedPin, OUTPUT);  // declare the
LED's pin as output

  for (x = 1; x <= 4; x++) {
    digitalWrite( LedPin, HIGH );
    delay(300);
    digitalWrite( LedPin, LOW );
    delay(300);
  }

  Serial.begin(31250);  //start serial with
midi baudrate 31250
  Serial.flush();

  MIDIchannel = EEPROM.read(0);
  MIDIchannel = MIDIchannel & 0x000F; // Only
channels 0 to 15

  octave = EEPROM.read(1);
  octave = octave & 0x000F; // Only channels 0
to 15
}

void loop() {

  // scan 13 switches on inputs
  for (int n = 0; n < 13; n++) {
    currentSwitch = digitalRead(switches[n]);

// switch pressed and NOT pressed previously
    if ( currentSwitch == LOW && switchState[n]
== LOW) {
```

```
      note = n;
      noteOn(MIDIchannel, note, velocity);
      switchState[n] = HIGH;
    }
// switch released and pressed previously
    if ( currentSwitch == HIGH &&
switchState[n] == HIGH ) {
      note = n;
      noteOff(MIDIchannel, note, velocity);
      switchState[n] = LOW;
    }
  }
  //-----------------------------------------------

// scan 2 Octave and MIDI Channel switches on
inputs
  for (int n = 13; n < 17; n++) {
    currentSwitch = digitalRead(switches[n]);

// switch pressed and NOT pressed previously
    if ( currentSwitch == LOW && switchState[n]
== LOW) {

      if (n == 13) {
        octave = octave + 12;
        if (octave >= 12) {
          octave = 12;
        }
        EEPROM.write(1, octave);
      }
      //---------------------
      if (n == 14) {
        octave = octave - 12;
        if (octave <= -12) {
          octave = -12;
        }
        EEPROM.write(1, octave);
      }
      //---------------------
      if (n == 15) {
        MIDIchannel = MIDIchannel + 1;
        if (MIDIchannel >= 15) {
          MIDIchannel = 15;
```

```
      }
      EEPROM.write(0, MIDIchannel);
    }
    //--------------------
    if (n == 16) {
      MIDIchannel = MIDIchannel - 1;
      if (MIDIchannel <= 0) {
        MIDIchannel = 0;
      }
      EEPROM.write(0, MIDIchannel);
    }
    //--------------------

    switchState[n] = HIGH;
    }
// switch released and pressed previously
    if ( currentSwitch == HIGH &&
switchState[n] == HIGH ) {
      switchState[n] = LOW;
    }
  }
  delay(20);
}

//---------------------------------------------

// Send a MIDI note-on message.
void noteOn(byte channel, byte note, byte
velocity) {
  midiMsg( (0x90 + channel), note + startNote +
octave, velocity);
}

// Send a MIDI note-off message.
void noteOff(byte channel, byte note, byte
velocity) {
  midiMsg( (0x80 + channel), note + startNote +
octave, velocity);
}

// Send a general MIDI message
void midiMsg(byte cmd, byte data1, byte data2)
{
```

```
  digitalWrite(LedPin, HIGH); // indicate we're
sending MIDI data
  Serial.write(cmd);
  Serial.write(data1);
  Serial.write(data2);
  digitalWrite(LedPin, LOW);
}
//----------------------------------------------
```

Listing 5: A 13 Note Bass Pedal Encoder with Octave and Channel Switches

9.4 Explanation of the Source Code

This program code is similar to the 13 Note Organ Bass Pedal Encoder, but with the addition of 4 switch inputs and the use of the internal Electronically Erasable Programmable Read Only Memory (EEPROM).

The EEPROM is used to store the values of the MIDI Octave and the MIDI Channel. It is called using the include statement:

```
#include <EEPROM.h>
```

The microcontroller on the Arduino board has EEPROM: memory whose values are kept when the board is turned off The EEPROM library enables you to read and write those bytes.

The supported micro-controllers on the various Arduino boards have different amounts of EEPROM: 1024 bytes on the ATmega328P, 512 bytes on the ATmega168 and ATmega8, 4 KB (4096 bytes) on the ATmega1280 and ATmega2560.

Full details on the EEPROM library are available at:

https://www.arduino.cc/en/Reference/EEPROM

When the program is switched on the EEPROM values are read:

```
MIDIchannel = EEPROM.read(0);
MIDIchannel = MIDIchannel & 0x000F; // Only
channels 0 to 15

octave = EEPROM.read(1);
octave = octave & 0x000F;
```

and stored into the MIDIchannel and octave variables.

While the program is running the extra 4 switches are scanned by:

```
// scan 2 Octave and MIDI Channel switches on
inputs
  for (int n = 13; n < 17; n++) {
    currentSwitch = digitalRead(switches[n]);

// switch pressed and NOT pressed previously
    if ( currentSwitch == LOW && switchState[n]
== LOW)
```

and if one of them is pressed the corresponding function is carried out. For example if '`if (n == 13)`' then the '`octave`' variable is increased by 12. However if you try to increase the '`octave`' by more than 12 it will remain at 12:

```
if (n == 13) {
  octave = octave + 12;
  if (octave >= 12) {
    octave = 12;
  }
  EEPROM.write(1, octave);
}
```

Also if '`if (n == 14)`' then the '`octave`' variable is decreased by -12. However if you try to decrease the '`octave`' by more than -12 it will remain at -12:

```
if (n == 14) {
  octave = octave - 12;
  if (octave <= -12) {
    octave = -12;
  }
  EEPROM.write(1, octave);
}
```

Also if '`if (n == 15)`' then the '`MIDIchannel`' variable is increased by 1. However if you try to increase the '`MIDIchannel`' by more than 15 it will remain at 15:

```
if (n == 15) {
  MIDIchannel = MIDIchannel + 1;
  if (MIDIchannel >= 15) {
    MIDIchannel = 15;
  }
  EEPROM.write(0, MIDIchannel);
}
```

Also if '`if (n == 16)`' then the 'MIDIchannel' variable is decreased by -1. However if you try to decrease the 'MIDIchannel' by more than 0 it will remain at 0:

```
if (n == 16) {
  MIDIchannel = MIDIchannel - 1;
  if (MIDIchannel <= 0) {
    MIDIchannel = 0;
  }
  EEPROM.write(0, MIDIchannel);
}
```

The result of any of the 4 switch changes is written to the EEPROM with the function: `EEPROM.write`

and after any switch is read the '`switchState[n]`' is set HIGH:

```
switchState[n] = HIGH;
```

When one of the switches is released and had been pressed previously the '`switchState[n]`' is set LOW:

```
// switch released and pressed previously
  if ( currentSwitch == HIGH && switchState[n]
== HIGH ) {
    switchState[n] = LOW;
  }
}
```

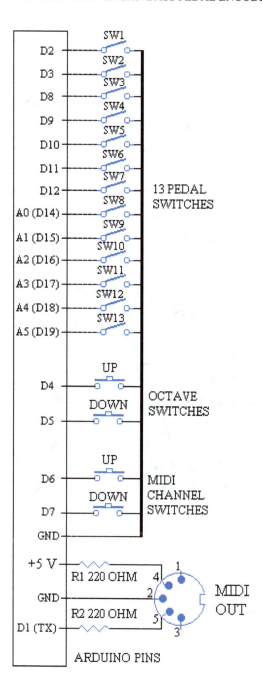

Figure 16: A 13 Note Bass Pedal Encoder with Octave and MIDI Channel Switches schematic

A 30 Note Organ Bass Pedal Encoder with MIDI IN/OUT

This design uses the Arduino UNO and the MIDI IN/OUT board. The MIDI Bass Pedal circuit is capable of encoding any number of momentary action, push to make, single pole single throw (SPST), switches from 1 up to 30 to produce the equivalent MIDI note-on/note-off data commands. The encoded switches are wired via IN4148 diodes. The keys are arranged in a (6x5) matrix for use with pedalboards with up to 30 switches. Any un-required switches can be left unconnected.

Figure 17: Arduino UNO with MIDI IN/OUT Board

The MIDI start Note is set to C2 (Note 36), but any different start note can be pre-programmed if required. The MIDI channel (1 to 16) is set using a 4-way DIP switch, see Table. The encoded switches are wired via IN4148 diodes.

10.1 Operation

This unit can work in standard MIDI Baud rate of 31250 This unit can be connected to new bass pedals or it can be used with an older non-MIDI bass pedals by using magnetic/reed switches to isolate the old and new scanning circuits. This will allow the older bass pedal synthesiser to continue to operate as normal while also providing a MIDI output. The design has a MIDI IN socket to allow MIDI merging with another MIDI source which produces a combined MIDI output. The system will also work with MIDI running status.

10.2 Organ Bass Pedal MIDI Wiring

The 30 switches are organized in a 6 x 5 matrix arrangement. But note if less than 30 switches are required, then ONLY the switches required need to be wired. The switch keys are wired as shown in the switches circuit schematic diagram.

The lowest note is switch 1 wired via diode D1 between Pins D8 and A1 (D15) of the Arduino. Pin D8 is also wired to the Anode of diode D7 and via SW7 to Pin A2 (D16) of the Arduino. Pin D8 is also wired to the Anode of diode D13 and via SW13 to Pin A3 (D17) of the Arduino. Pin D8 is also wired to the Anode of diode D19 and via SW19 to Pin A4 (D18) of the Arduino.

Arduino pin terminal connected to A1 (D15) is wired to one side of the 6 key switches SW1 to SW6, and the wire can be looped from one key switch to the next. Arduino pin terminal connected to A2 (D16) is wired to one side of the 6 key switches SW7 to SW12. Arduino pin terminal connected to A3 (D17) is wired to one side of the 6 key switches SW13 to SW18.

Arduino pin terminal connected to A4 (D18) is wired to one side of the 6 key switches SW19 to SW24. Each of the other side of these switches SW1 to SW6 is wired to a diode on the Cathode (K) side (end of diode with stripe).The other side of each of these diodes is looped to 4 other diodes. For example Anode (A) of diode D1 is looped to D7 then to D13 then to D19. The rest of the wiring is done in a similar manner.

10.3 MIDI Channel Selection

The MIDI Channel (1-16) is user selectable via the 4-way DIP switch

DIP Switch Selections				MIDI Channel
4	3	2	1	
on	on	on	on	1
on	on	on	off	2
on	on	off	on	3
on	on	off	off	4
on	off	on	on	5
on	off	on	off	6
on	off	off	on	7
on	off	off	off	8
off	on	on	on	9
off	on	on	off	10
off	on	off	on	11
off	on	off	off	12
off	off	on	on	13
off	off	on	off	14
off	off	off	on	15
off	off	off	off	16
MIDI Channel Selection				

Table 5: MIDI Channel Selection

10.4 Features

The MIDI 30 NOTE BASS PEDAL ENCODER Unit consists of an Arduino UNO board, the velocity byte is preset to a value of 100, the MIDI start Note is set to C2 (Note 36), the MIDI channel (1-16) is user selectable via the 4-way DIP switch, a 2.1mm power socket, and associated power LED, a MIDI detection LED, a MIDI In/Out Board, a 150mm wired MIDI 5-pin DIN input socket, a 150mm wired MIDI 5-pin DIN output socket. a 9v battery or equivalent DC power source or powered via the USB socket, 30 Suitable key-switches or magnetic reed switches and associated IN4148 diodes.

10.5 Source Code for the 30 Note Organ Bass Pedal MIDI Encoder

```
// Program to read 30 switches in 6x5 matrix

#include <MIDI.h>
MIDI_CREATE_DEFAULT_INSTANCE();

// define the output pins we use
#define cols0 15
#define cols1 16
#define cols2 17
#define cols3 18
#define cols4 19

// Constants
#define ROW0 8
#define ROW1 9
#define ROW2 10
#define ROW3 11
#define ROW4 12
#define ROW5 14
```

```
#define LedPin      13  // for midi out status

byte rows[6] = {
  ROW0, ROW1, ROW2, ROW3, ROW4, ROW5
};

byte MIDIchannel;
byte noteFlag;
byte count;
byte firstNote = 36;
byte countNote;
byte Last = 30;
byte KeyFlags[30];
byte velocity = 100;
byte val, row, Key, i, x, note;

void setup() {

  pinMode(2, OUTPUT);
  pinMode(3, OUTPUT);
// GND 0 Volt supply to opto-coupler
  digitalWrite(3, LOW);
 // +5 Volt supply to opto-coupler
  digitalWrite(2, HIGH);

 // Set Inputs for 4 way DIP Switch
  pinMode(4, INPUT_PULLUP);
  pinMode(5, INPUT_PULLUP);
  pinMode(6, INPUT_PULLUP);
  pinMode(7, INPUT_PULLUP);

  pinMode(cols0, OUTPUT); // Columns Outputs x5
  pinMode(cols1, OUTPUT);
  pinMode(cols2, OUTPUT);
  pinMode(cols3, OUTPUT);
  pinMode(cols4, OUTPUT);

  pinMode(ROW0, INPUT_PULLUP); // Row Inputs x6
  pinMode(ROW1, INPUT_PULLUP);
  pinMode(ROW2, INPUT_PULLUP);
  pinMode(ROW3, INPUT_PULLUP);
  pinMode(ROW4, INPUT_PULLUP);
  pinMode(ROW5, INPUT_PULLUP);
```

```
  // Initialise Flags to 00
  for (i = 0; i < Last; i++) {
    KeyFlags[i] = 0;
  }

  countNote = 0;

  pinMode(LedPin, OUTPUT);
  MIDI.begin(MIDI_CHANNEL_OMNI);
}
//---------------------------------------------

void loop() {

  MIDI.read();

  // Read 4-way DIP switch
  MIDIchannel = digitalRead(4) +
(digitalRead(5) << 1) + (digitalRead(6) << 2) +
(digitalRead(7) << 3);
  MIDIchannel = MIDIchannel + 1;

  digitalWrite(cols0, LOW);
  digitalWrite(cols1, HIGH);
  digitalWrite(cols2, HIGH);
  digitalWrite(cols3, HIGH);
  digitalWrite(cols4, HIGH);

  readRow();
  digitalWrite(cols0, HIGH);
  digitalWrite(cols1, LOW);
  readRow();
  digitalWrite(cols1, HIGH);
  digitalWrite(cols2, LOW);
  readRow();
  digitalWrite(cols2, HIGH);
  digitalWrite(cols3, LOW);
  readRow();
  digitalWrite(cols3, HIGH);
  digitalWrite(cols4, LOW);
  readRow();
  digitalWrite(cols4, HIGH);
```

```
  delay(20); // Delay for switch debounce
}

//------------------------------------------------

void readRow() {
  for (x = 0; x < 6; x++) {
    Key = !(digitalRead(rows[x]));
    noteFlag = (KeyFlags[countNote]);

    if (Key && !noteFlag) { // 1 0
      note = countNote + firstNote;
      MIDI.sendNoteOn(note, velocity,
  MIDIchannel);
      KeyFlags[countNote] = HIGH; //Set Flag
    }

    else if (!Key && noteFlag) { // 0 1
      note = countNote + firstNote;
      MIDI.sendNoteOff(note, velocity,
  MIDIchannel);
      KeyFlags[countNote] = LOW; //Clear Flag
    }

    countNote++;
    if (countNote == Last)
      countNote = 0;
  }
}
```

Listing 6: Code for a 30 (6x5) Note Organ Bass Pedal

10.6 Explanation of the Source Code

The lines:

```
#include <MIDI.h>
MIDI_CREATE_DEFAULT_INSTANCE();
```

call the MIDI Library functions and initialises MIDI with:

```
MIDI.begin(MIDI_CHANNEL_OMNI);
```

For the MIDI IN/OUT board, Pins D0 and D1 are connected to the RX and TX pins, respectively. Arduino Pins D2 and D3 require +5 Volt and 0 Volt(GND), respectively, and these voltages are provided in the software with these lines:

```
  pinMode(2, OUTPUT);
  pinMode(3, OUTPUT);
// GND 0 Volt supply to opto-coupler
  digitalWrite(3, LOW);
 // +5 Volt supply to opto-coupler
  digitalWrite(2, HIGH);
```

Finally you need to set Arduino Pins D4, D5, D6 and D7, as digital input pins with internal pull-up resistors. These are connected to the 4-way DIL switch, to select the MIDI Channel (1 to 16), with these lines:

```
 // Set Inputs for 4 way DIP Switch
  pinMode(4, INPUT_PULLUP);
  pinMode(5, INPUT_PULLUP);
  pinMode(6, INPUT_PULLUP);
  pinMode(7, INPUT_PULLUP);
```

The Columns are set to Outputs, and the Rows are set to Inputs with the internal pullup input resistor using:

```
pinMode(cols0, OUTPUT); // Columns Outputs x5
pinMode(cols1, OUTPUT);
pinMode(cols2, OUTPUT);
pinMode(cols3, OUTPUT);
pinMode(cols4, OUTPUT);

pinMode(ROW0, INPUT_PULLUP); // Row Inputs x6
pinMode(ROW1, INPUT_PULLUP);
pinMode(ROW2, INPUT_PULLUP);
pinMode(ROW3, INPUT_PULLUP);
pinMode(ROW4, INPUT_PULLUP);
pinMode(ROW5, INPUT_PULLUP);
```

The Flags for all the switches are initialised to 0 using:

```
// Initialise Flags to 00
for (i = 0; i < Last; i++) {
  KeyFlags[i] = 0;
}
```

The void loop() starts by reading the MIDI Input using:

```
MIDI.read();
```

this function reads the input MIDI data and merges it with the internal 30 Note encoder data, then sends the combined data to the MIDI OUT socket.

The 4-way DIP switches are read, shifted and added to produce a sum between 0 and 15 for the MIDI Channel. However the Arduino MIDI Library software requires MIDI Channel values between 1 to 16. So 1 is added to the 'MIDIchannel' variable, as shown in this section of code:

```
// Read 4-way DIP switch
```

```
MIDIchannel = digitalRead(4) + (digitalRead(5)
<< 1) + (digitalRead(6) << 2) + (digitalRead(7)
<< 3);
MIDIchannel = MIDIchannel + 1;
```

The Columns and Rows are read sequentially. Each Column is set LOW in turn and then the Rows are read:

```
digitalWrite(cols0, LOW);
digitalWrite(cols1, HIGH);
digitalWrite(cols2, HIGH);
digitalWrite(cols3, HIGH);
digitalWrite(cols4, HIGH);

readRow();
digitalWrite(cols0, HIGH);
digitalWrite(cols1, LOW);
readRow();
digitalWrite(cols1, HIGH);
digitalWrite(cols2, LOW);
readRow();
digitalWrite(cols2, HIGH);
digitalWrite(cols3, LOW);
readRow();
digitalWrite(cols3, HIGH);
digitalWrite(cols4, LOW);
readRow();
digitalWrite(cols4, HIGH);
```

The six Rows are read using a FOR Loop:

```
for (x = 0; x < 6; x++) {
```

which reads the 'Key' and the 'noteFlag' variables:

```
Key = !(digitalRead(rows[x]));
noteFlag = (KeyFlags[countNote]);
```

If a key is pressed and the noteFlag is 0:

```
if (Key && !noteFlag) { // 1 0
   note = countNote + firstNote;
   MIDI.sendNoteOn(note, velocity,
MIDIchannel);
   KeyFlags[countNote] = HIGH; //Set Flag
}
```

Then the note is equal to the countNote + firstNote and the Note On command is transmitted to the MIDI Output

Else if a key is released and the noteFlag is set :

```
else if (!Key && noteFlag) { // 0 1
   note = countNote + firstNote;
   MIDI.sendNoteOff(note, velocity,
MIDIchannel);
   KeyFlags[countNote] = LOW; //Clear Flag
}
```

Then the note is equal to the countNote + firstNote and the Note Off command is transmitted to the MIDI Output

10.7 The 30 (6x5) Note Organ Bass Pedal Circuit Schematic Diagram

The 30 Note Organ Bass Pedal Schematic circuit diagram is divided into two sections showing the wiring for switches 1 to 18 and then switches 19 to 30. The 8 connections labelled A to H are joined to each other, to form the complete 30 (6x5) note circuit.

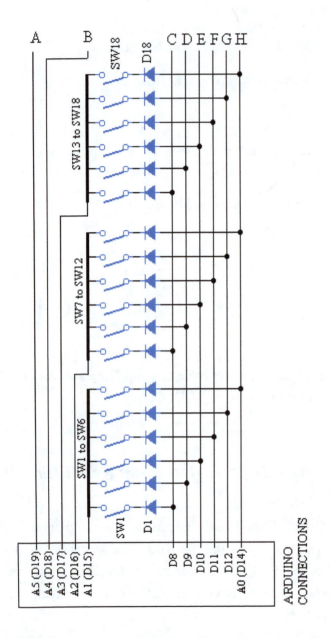

Figure 18: A 30 Note Organ Bass Pedal Encoder with Switches 1 to 18

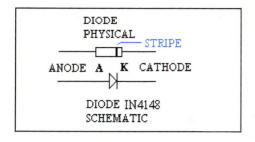

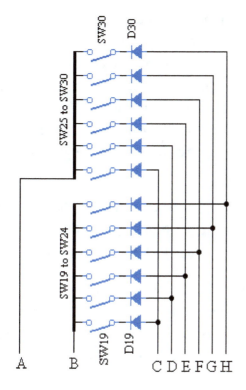

Figure 19: A 30 Note Organ Bass Pedal Encoder with Switches 19 to 30

A MIDI 32 (8x4) Note Organ Bass Pedal Encoder with MIDI Thru

This design uses an Arduino UNO board and the MIDI OUT hardware. This MIDI Bass Pedal Encoder circuit, arranged in an 8x4 matrix, is capable of encoding up to 32 momentary action, push to make, single pole single throw (SPST), switches to produce the equivalent MIDI note-on/note-off data commands. There are also Octave Up and Octave Down switch inputs and MIDI Channel Up and Down switch inputs. The Octave and MIDI Channel are stored into non-volatile EEPROM memory. So when the unit is powered up the previous Octave MIDI Channel selections that were used are restored. Note that if the MIDI Octave or MIDI Channel switches are not required, they can be left unconnected.

The encoded switches are wired via IN4148 diodes. The keys are arranged in a matrix for use with pedalboards with up to 32 switches. Any unrequired switches can be left unconnected.

The MIDI start Note is set to C2 (MIDI Note 36), which is connected to switch SW1, then the switches follow continuously to the last switch SW32, which is G4 (MIDI Note 67). But any different start note can be pre-programmed if required.

11.1 Operation

This unit can work in standard MIDI Baud rate of 31250. This unit can be connected to new bass pedals or it can be used with an older non-MIDI bass pedals by using magnetic/reed switches to isolate the old and new scanning circuits. This will allow the older bass pedal synthesiser to continue to operate as normal while also providing a MIDI output.

11.2 Features

The MIDI 32 Note Bass Pedal Encoder Unit consists of a MIDI Arduino Board, the velocity byte is preset to a value of 100, the start note of the bass pedal encoder is from MIDI note C2 (MIDI Note 36), Octave Up and Octave Down switch inputs, the Octave selection is stored into non-volatile EEPROM memory, MIDI Channel Up and MIDI Channel Down switch inputs, the MIDI Channel is stored into non-volatile EEPROM memory, a 2.1mm power socket, and associated power LED, a MIDI 5-pin DIN output socket and associated series resistors, a 9v battery or equivalent DC power source or powered via the USB socket, 32 suitable key-switches or magnetic reed switches, suitable 2 momentary action Octave Up/Down switches, suitable 2 momentary action MIDI Channel Up/Down switches.

11.3 Source Code for the 32 (8x4) Note Organ Bass Pedal MIDI Encoder

```
//PROGRAM: A design with a 32 (8x4) switch
encoder circuit,
// with Octave and Channel UP/DOWN switches, to
produce Bass pedal outputs

#include <EEPROM.h>

// define the output pins we use
#define cols0 10
#define cols1 11
#define cols2 12
#define cols3 14

byte switches[4] = {
  15, 16, 17, 18
};
```

```
byte switchState[4] = {
  0, 0, 0, 0
};

byte currentSwitch = 0;
int octave = 0;
int MIDIchannel = 2; // midi channel 3
byte LedPin = 13;
byte noteOn = 0x90;
byte noteOff = 0x80;
byte noteFlag;
byte countNote = 0;
byte Last = 32;
byte KeyFlags[32];
byte velocity = 100;
byte row, Key, x, note;
int startNote = 36;

void setup() {
// Columns Outputs x4
  pinMode(cols0, OUTPUT);
  pinMode(cols1, OUTPUT);
  pinMode(cols2, OUTPUT);
  pinMode(cols3, OUTPUT);
// Row Inputs x8 Switch Matrix 8x4 = 32
switches
  pinMode(2, INPUT_PULLUP);
  pinMode(3, INPUT_PULLUP);
  pinMode(4, INPUT_PULLUP);
  pinMode(5, INPUT_PULLUP);
  pinMode(6, INPUT_PULLUP);
  pinMode(7, INPUT_PULLUP);
  pinMode(8, INPUT_PULLUP);
  pinMode(9, INPUT_PULLUP);
// Octave + MIDI Channel switch inputs
  pinMode(15, INPUT_PULLUP);
  pinMode(16, INPUT_PULLUP);
  pinMode(17, INPUT_PULLUP);
  pinMode(18, INPUT_PULLUP);
// declare the LED's pin as output
  pinMode(LedPin, OUTPUT);
```

```
   for (x = 1; x <= 4; x++) {
     digitalWrite( LedPin, HIGH );
     delay(300);
     digitalWrite( LedPin, LOW );
     delay(300);
   }
//start serial with midi baudrate 31250
   Serial.begin(31250);
   Serial.flush();

   MIDIchannel = EEPROM.read(0);
   MIDIchannel = MIDIchannel & 0x000F;
   octave = EEPROM.read(1);
   octave = octave & 0x000F;
}
//-----------------------------------------------
void loop() {

   digitalWrite(cols0, LOW);
   digitalWrite(cols1, HIGH);
   digitalWrite(cols2, HIGH);
   digitalWrite(cols3, HIGH);

   readRow();
   digitalWrite(cols0, HIGH);
   digitalWrite(cols1, LOW);
   readRow();
   digitalWrite(cols1, HIGH);
   digitalWrite(cols2, LOW);
   readRow();
   digitalWrite(cols2, HIGH);
   digitalWrite(cols3, LOW);
   readRow();
   digitalWrite(cols3, HIGH);

//-----------------------------------------------

// scan 2 Octave and MIDI Channel switches on
inputs
   for (int n = 0; n < 4; n++) {
     currentSwitch = digitalRead(switches[n]);

     // switch pressed and NOT pressed
```

```
previously
    if ( currentSwitch == LOW && switchState[n]
== LOW) {
      //---------------
      if (n == 0) {
        octave = octave + 12;
        if (octave >= 12) {
          octave = 12;
        }
        EEPROM.write(1, octave);
      }
      //--------------------
      if (n == 1) {
        octave = octave - 12;
        if (octave <= -12) {
          octave = -12;
        }
        EEPROM.write(1, octave);
      }
      //--------------------
      if (n == 2) {
        MIDIchannel = MIDIchannel + 1;
        if (MIDIchannel >= 15) {
          MIDIchannel = 15;
        }
        EEPROM.write(0, MIDIchannel);
      }
      //--------------------
      if (n == 3) {
        MIDIchannel = MIDIchannel - 1;
        if (MIDIchannel <= 0) {
          MIDIchannel = 0;
        }
        EEPROM.write(0, MIDIchannel);
      }
      //--------------------

      switchState[n] = HIGH;
    }

    // switch released and pressed previously
    if ( currentSwitch == HIGH &&
switchState[n] == HIGH ) {
```

```
              switchState[n] = LOW;
        }
    }
    delay(20);
}
//-----------------------------------------------
// Send a general MIDI message
void midiSend(byte cmd, byte data1, byte data2)
{
    digitalWrite(LedPin, HIGH);
    Serial.write(cmd);
    Serial.write(data1);
    Serial.write(data2);
    digitalWrite(LedPin, LOW);
}
//-----------------------------------------------
void readRow() {
    for (row = 2; row <= 9; row++) {
        Key = !(digitalRead(row));
        noteFlag = (KeyFlags[countNote]);

        if (Key && !noteFlag) { // 1 0
            note = countNote + startNote + octave;
            midiSend( noteOn + MIDIchannel, note,
velocity);
            KeyFlags[countNote] = HIGH; //Set Flag
        }

        else if (!Key && noteFlag) { // 0 1
            note = countNote + startNote + octave;
            midiSend(noteOff + MIDIchannel, note,
velocity);
            KeyFlags[countNote] = LOW; //Clear Flag
        }

        countNote++;
        if (countNote == Last)
            countNote = 0;
    }
}
```

Listing 7: Code for a 32 (8x4) Note Organ Bass Pedal Encoder

11.4 Explanation of the Source Code

This program makes use of the internal Electronically Erasable Programmable Read Only Memory (EEPROM).

The EEPROM is used to store the values of the MIDI Octave and the MIDI Channel. It is called using the include statement:

```
#include <EEPROM.h>
```

The microcontroller on the Arduino board has EEPROM: memory whose values are kept when the board is turned off The EEPROM library enables you to read and write those bytes.

This project has the 32 switches arranged in an 8x4 matrix. The 4 Columns are setup as Outputs:

```
// Columns Outputs x4
  pinMode(cols0, OUTPUT);
  pinMode(cols1, OUTPUT);
  pinMode(cols2, OUTPUT);
  pinMode(cols3, OUTPUT);
```

and the 8 Rows are setup as Inputs with the internal Pullup resistor selected::

```
// Row Inputs x8 Switch Matrix 8x4 = 32 switches
  pinMode(2, INPUT_PULLUP);
  pinMode(3, INPUT_PULLUP);
  pinMode(4, INPUT_PULLUP);
  pinMode(5, INPUT_PULLUP);
  pinMode(6, INPUT_PULLUP);
  pinMode(7, INPUT_PULLUP);
  pinMode(8, INPUT_PULLUP);
  pinMode(9, INPUT_PULLUP);
```

and the Octave and MIDI Channel Pins are setup as Inputs with the internal Pullup resistor selected:

```
// Octave + MIDI Channel switch inputs
  pinMode(15, INPUT_PULLUP);
  pinMode(16, INPUT_PULLUP);
  pinMode(17, INPUT_PULLUP);
  pinMode(18, INPUT_PULLUP);
// declare the LED's pin as output
```

The Columns and Rows are read sequentially. Each Column is set LOW in turn and then the Rows are read:

```
digitalWrite(cols0, LOW);
digitalWrite(cols1, HIGH);
digitalWrite(cols2, HIGH);
digitalWrite(cols3, HIGH);

readRow();
digitalWrite(cols0, HIGH);
digitalWrite(cols1, LOW);
readRow();
digitalWrite(cols1, HIGH);
digitalWrite(cols2, LOW);
readRow();
digitalWrite(cols2, HIGH);
digitalWrite(cols3, LOW);
readRow();
digitalWrite(cols3, HIGH);
```

The Octave and MIDI Channel selection using the EEPROM works in a similar manner to the previous project.

11.5 The 32 (8x4) Note Organ Bass Pedal Circuit Schematic Diagram

The 32 (8x4) Note Organ Bass Pedal Schematic circuit diagram is divided into two sections showing the wiring for switches 0 to 15 and then switches 16 to 31. The 10 connections labelled A to J are joined to each other, to form the complete 32 (8x4) note circuit.

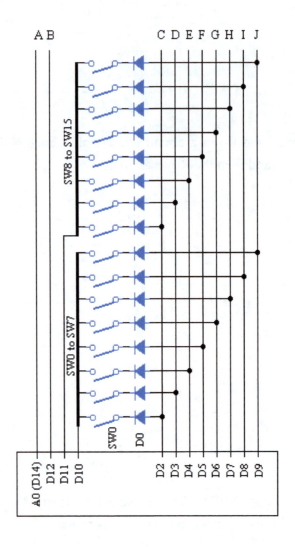

Figure 20: A 32 (8x4) Note Organ Bass Pedal Encoder Switches 0 to 15

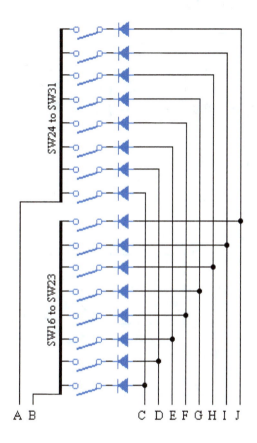

Figure 21: A 32 (8x4) Note Organ Bass Pedal Encoder Switches 16 to 31

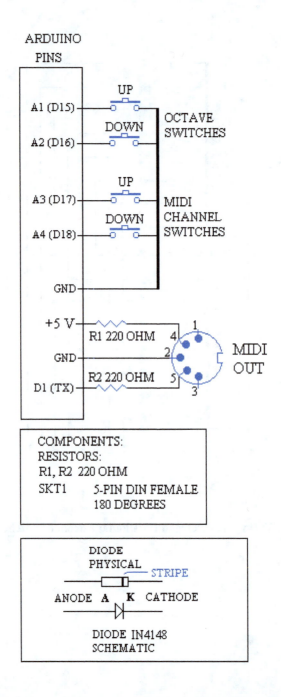

Figure 22: A 32 (8x4) Note Organ Bass Pedal Encoder with Octave and MIDI Channel Switches

A 32 Note Organ Bass Pedal MIDI Encoder with Octave and MIDI Channel selection

This design uses an Arduino MEGA 2560 board and the MIDI OUT hardware. The MIDI Bass Pedal Encoder circuit is capable of encoding up to 32 momentary action, push to make, single pole single throw (SPST), switches to produce the equivalent MIDI note-on/note-off data commands.

Figure 23: An Arduino Mega 2560 Board with MIDI OUT Socket

So this design can be used with any 13 up to 32 note pedalboards. Any unrequired notes can just be left unconnected. There are also

Octave Up and Octave Down switch inputs. These can be left unconnected if not required.

12.1 Operation

One side of each of the encoded Bass Pedal switches are wired to a common Ground (GND) pin and the other side of the switches 1 to 32 are wired to the digital input pins 22 to 53, respectively. The MIDI start Note is set to C2 (MIDI Note 36), which is connected to switch SW1, then the switches follow continuously to the last switch SW32, which is G4 (MIDI Note 67). But any different start note can be pre-programmed if required. This unit can work in the standard MIDI Baud rate of 31250

12.2 Features

The MIDI 32 Note Bass Pedal Encoder Unit consists of an a MIDI Arduino Mega 2560 Board, the MIDI channel is preset to channel 3, the velocity byte is preset to a value of 100, the start note of the bass pedal encoder is from MIDI note C2 (MIDI Note 36), Octave Up and Octave Down switch inputs, a 2.1mm power socket, and associated power LED, a MIDI 5-pin DIN output socket and associated series resistors, a 9v battery or equivalent DC power source or powered via the USB socket, 32 suitable key-switches or magnetic reed switches, 2 suitable momentary action Octave up/down switches.

12.3 Source Code for the 32 (32x1) Note Organ Bass Pedal MIDI Encoder

```
// PROGRAM: A design with an 32 switch encoder
circuit, to produce Bass pedal outputs,
// with Octave UP/DOWN switches.
```

```
//variables setup
int octave = 0;
int midiByte;
byte MIDIchannel = 2; // midi channel 3
byte channel;
byte x;
byte LedPin = 13;    // select the pin for the
LED
byte count;
byte note;
byte velocity = 100;
byte currentSwitch = 0;
int startNote = 36;

// 32 bass switches + octave and Channel up +
octave down switches  = 36 switch inputs-
byte switches[36] = {
  22, 23, 24, 25, 26, 27, 28, 29, 30, 31, 32,
33, 34, 35, 36, 37, 38, 39, 40, 41,
  42, 43, 44, 45, 46, 47, 48, 49, 50, 51, 52,
53, 8, 9, 10, 11
};

byte switchState[36] = {
  0, 0, 0, 0, 0, 0, 0, 0, 0, 0, 0, 0, 0, 0, 0,
0, 0, 0, 0, 0,
  0, 0, 0, 0, 0, 0, 0, 0, 0, 0, 0, 0, 0, 0, 0,
0
};

//-----------------------------------------------

void setup() {

// Set Inputs for Octave up/down Switches
  pinMode(8, INPUT_PULLUP);
  pinMode(9, INPUT_PULLUP);
// Set Inputs for Channel up/down Switches
  pinMode(10, INPUT_PULLUP);
  pinMode(11, INPUT_PULLUP);

  // pins 22 to 53 corresponding to switches 1
to 32
```

```
  for (x = 22; x < 54; x++) {
    pinMode(x, INPUT);
    digitalWrite(x, HIGH);
  }

 // declare the LED's pin as output
  pinMode(LedPin, OUTPUT);

  for (x = 1; x <= 4; x++) {
    digitalWrite( LedPin, HIGH );
    delay(300);
    digitalWrite( LedPin, LOW );
    delay(300);
  }

 //start serial with midi baudrate 31250
  Serial.begin(31250);
  Serial.flush();
}
//-----------------------------------------------
void loop() {

  // scan 32 switches on inputs
  for (int n = 0; n < 32; n++) {
    currentSwitch = digitalRead(switches[n]);

    // switch pressed and NOT pressed
previously
    if ( currentSwitch == LOW && switchState[n]
== LOW) {

      switchState[n] = HIGH;
      note = n;
      noteOn(MIDIchannel, note, velocity);
    }

    // switch released AND pressed previously
    if ( currentSwitch == HIGH &&
switchState[n] == HIGH ) {

      switchState[n] = LOW;
      note = n;
      noteOff(MIDIchannel, note, velocity);
```

```
      }
    }
  //----------------------------------------------

  // scan 2 Octave and Channel switches on
inputs
  for (int n = 32; n < 36; n++) {
    currentSwitch = digitalRead(switches[n]);

    // switch pressed and NOT pressed
previously
    if ( currentSwitch == LOW && switchState[n]
== LOW) {
      //---------------
      if (n == 32) {
        octave = octave + 12;
        if (octave >= 12) {
          octave = 12;
        }
      }
      //--------------------
      if (n == 33) {
        octave = octave - 12;
        if (octave <= -12) {
          octave = -12;
        }
      }
      //--------------------
      if (n == 34) {
        MIDIchannel = MIDIchannel + 1;
        if (MIDIchannel >= 15) {
          MIDIchannel = 15;
        }
      }
      //--------------------
      if (n == 35) {
        MIDIchannel = MIDIchannel - 1;
        if (MIDIchannel <= 0) {
          MIDIchannel = 0;
        }
      }

      switchState[n] = HIGH;
```

```
    }

    // switch released AND pressed previously
    if ( currentSwitch == HIGH &&
switchState[n] == HIGH ) {

      switchState[n] = LOW;
    }

  }
  delay(20);
}

// ---------------------------------------------

// Send a MIDI note-on message.
void noteOn(byte channel, byte note, byte
velocity) {
  midiMsg( (0x90 + channel), note + startNote +
octave, velocity);
}

// Send a MIDI note-off message.
void noteOff(byte channel, byte note, byte
velocity) {
  midiMsg( (0x80 + channel), note + startNote +
octave, velocity);
}

// Send a general MIDI message
void midiMsg(byte cmd, byte data1, byte data2)
{
  digitalWrite(LedPin, HIGH);
  Serial.write(cmd);
  Serial.write(data1);
  Serial.write(data2);
  digitalWrite(LedPin, LOW);
}
//---------------------------------------------
```

Listing 8: Code for a 32 (32x1) Note Organ Bass Pedal Encoder

12.4 Explanation of the Source Code

There are two Arrays each with 36 memory locations. One group is for the 36 switches and the second is for 36 Flag switches, which are all preset to zero:

```
// 32 bass switches + octave and Channel up +
octave down switches  = 36 switch inputs-
byte switches[36] = {
  22, 23, 24, 25, 26, 27, 28, 29, 30, 31, 32, 33,
34, 35, 36, 37, 38, 39, 40, 41,
  42, 43, 44, 45, 46, 47, 48, 49, 50, 51, 52, 53,
8, 9, 10, 11
};

byte switchState[36] = {
  0, 0, 0, 0, 0, 0, 0, 0, 0, 0, 0, 0, 0, 0, 0, 0,
0, 0, 0, 0,
  0, 0, 0, 0, 0, 0, 0, 0, 0, 0, 0, 0, 0, 0, 0, 0
};
```

The Octave and MIDIchannel Pins are set to Inputs with the internal Pullup resistor selected:

```
// Set Inputs for Octave up/down Switches
  pinMode(8, INPUT_PULLUP);
  pinMode(9, INPUT_PULLUP);
// Set Inputs for Channel up/down Switches
  pinMode(10, INPUT_PULLUP);
  pinMode(11, INPUT_PULLUP);
```

and pins 22 to 53 corresponding to switches 1 to 32 are set to Inputs with the internal Pullup resistor selected:

```
// pins 22 to 53 corresponding to switches 1 to
32
  for (x = 22; x < 54; x++) {
```

```
pinMode(x, INPUT);
digitalWrite(x, HIGH);
}
```

The switch selection and MIDI Out functions operate in a similar manner to the software code in the previous projects.

12.5 The 32 (32x1) Note Organ Bass Pedal Schematic Diagram

One side of all the switches is connected to the Arduino Ground (GND) Pin, and the other side of each of the switches is connected to individual Pins on the Arduino board. Also the GND label in the diagram for switches 1 to 16 is connected to the GND Pin in the diagram for the switches 17 to 32.

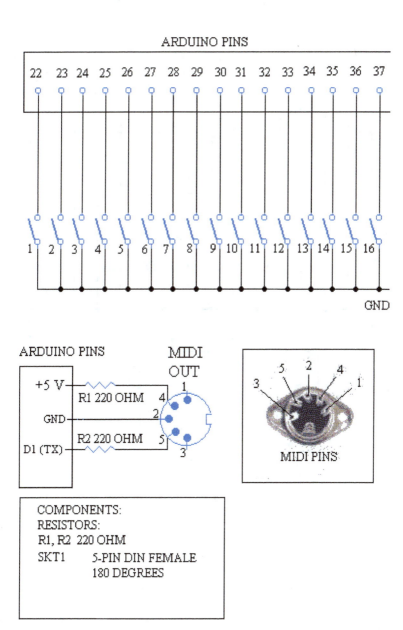

Figure 24: A 32 Note Organ Bass Pedal Encoder with Switches 1 to 16

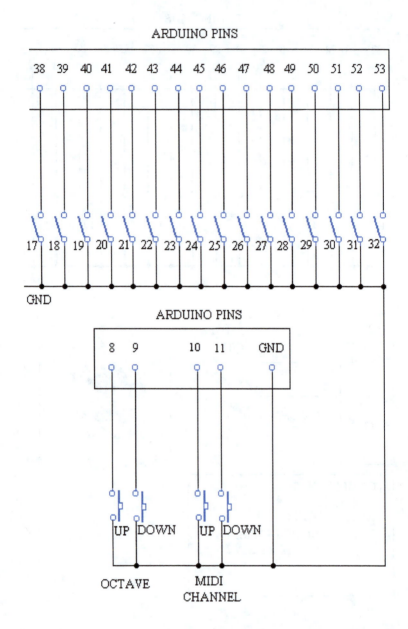

Figure 25: A 32 Note Organ Bass Pedal Encoder Switches 17 to 32 and Octave and MIDI Channel Switches

About the Author

Tom Scarff, founder of MIDI Music Kits, has been working in the Electronics Industry for more than 35 years. He spent nearly 15 years working in electronic maintenance, design and development in the Irish national broadcasting organisation, RTE. More recently he has been employed in the Dublin Institute of Technology, DIT (now the Technological University of Dublin, TUD) lecturing in Computer and Electronic Engineering and in Music Technology. He has also published a number of articles on topics including audio, music and MIDI in particular.

He has designed and produced a number of MIDI circuit designs using the ATmega series of micro-controllers. The designs are based on the Arduino and are compatible with the open-source IDE, which can be downloaded for free (currently for Mac OS X, Windows, and Linux).

He has spent many years working in the development and design of electronic music, building many different types of MIDI musical instruments. He saw how difficult it was to create simple MIDI instruments and he wanted to create something that makes it easier for people to create, build, connect and enjoy making their own musical instruments.

The author can be contacted via his website at:

https://www.midikits.net/

ρ

www.ingramcontent.com/pod-product-compliance
Lightning Source LLC
La Vergne TN
LVHW051642050326
832903LV00022B/850